REVOLUTIONARY PENSIONERS

A TRANSCRIPT OF THE PENSION LIST

OF

THE UNITED STATES

FOR

1813

CLEARFIELD

Originally published
1813

Reprinted for
Clearfield Company, Inc. by
Genealogical Publishing Co., Inc.
Baltimore, Maryland
1990, 1994, 1995, 1996, 1997, 2002

International Standard Book Number: 0-8063-4538-1

Made in the United States of America

LETTER

FROM

THE SECRETARY OF WAR,

COMMUNICATING

A TRANSCRIPT OF THE PENSION LIST

OF

𝕿𝖍𝖊 𝖀𝖓𝖎𝖙𝖊𝖉 𝕾𝖙𝖆𝖙𝖊𝖘,

SHEWING THE

NUMBER OF PENSIONERS IN THE SEVERAL DISTRICTS.

ALSO,

THE AMOUNT ALLOWED TO EACH PENSIONER.

———————

JUNE 1, 1813.

Referred to the Committee of Claims.

———————

WASHINGTON:

A. AND G. WAY, PRINTERS.

••••••••••••••
1813.

WASHINGTON CITY,

May 31*st*, 1813.

SIR,

I HAVE the honor to transmit you herewith, to be laid before the House, a report relative to the pension list of the United States.

I have the honor to be,

Sir,

Very respectfully,

Your obedient servant,

JOHN ARMSTRONG.

To the Hon. the speaker
of the House of Representatives
of the United States.

WAR DEPARTMENT,

May 28th, 1813.

IN obedience to a resolution of the House of Representatives of the United States, bearing date the 12th of February, 1812, the Secretary of War has the honor to present a transcript of the pension list of the said states, (contained on four sheets in folio, paged from one to sixteen) exhibiting the number of each pensioner as he stands on the roll of the respective districts or agencies, his rank or quality, and the amount of the annual stipend at present allowed each person by law.

All which is respectfully submitted.

JOHN ARMSTRONG.

SCHEDULE of the Names, Rank and Annual Stipends of the Invalids, Pensioners of the United States.

District or Agency.	No. on the Roll.	NAMES.	Rank or Quality.	Annual Stipend.
New Hampshire,	1	Peter Akerman,	private,	40
	2	Andrew Aikin,	sergt. major,	45
	3	Caleb Aldrish,	sergeant,	60
	4	Caleb Austin,	private,	20
	5	Daniel Buzzle,	do.	60
	6	Archelaus Batchelor,	sergeant,	30
	7	Ebenezer Bean,	private,	20
	8	Francis Blood,	do.	60
	9	James Cobby,	do.	(dead)
	10	James Campbell,	do.	48
	11	Nathaniel Church,	do.	60
	12	Ebenezer Carleton,	do.	60
	13	Levi Chubbuck,	fifer,	45
	14	Morrel Coburn,	private,	15
	15	William Curtiss,	do.	60
	16	James Crummitt,	do.	60
	17	Jabez Church,	do.	30
	18	Benjamin Cotton,	do.	30
	19	David Duncan,	do.	40
	20	Henry Danforth,	do.	30
	21	James Dean,	do.	15
	22	Lemuel Dean,	do.	60
	23	Francis Davidson,	do.	48
	24	Edward Evans,	do.	60
	25	Thomas Eastman,	do.	45
	26	Ebenezer Fletcher,	fifer,	15
	27	Stephen Fuller,	private,	20
	28	James Gould,	lieutenant,	160
	29	Abner Gage,	private,	60
	30	Moses S. George,	do.	30
	31	Joshua Gilman,	do.	40
	32	Windsor Gleason,	do.	15
	33	Joseph Greely,	do.	15
	34	Joseph Green,	do.	30
	35	Jonas Green,	do.	60
	36	William Hastings,	do.	60
	37	Thomas Haynes,	do.	60
	38	Joshua Haynes,	do.	48
	39	Nathan Holt,	do.	15
	40	Charles Huntoon, junior,	do.	20
	41	Zadock Hurd,	do.	20
	42	Joseph Hilton,	lieutenant,	80
	43	Jonathan Holton,	do.	120
	44	James Hawkley,	private,	60
	45	Ebenezer Jennings,	sergeant,	15
	46	Peter Johnson,	private,	15
	47	Benjamin Jenkins,	sergeant,	30
	48	Abraham Kimball,	private,	30
	49	Benjamin Knight,	sergeant,	20
	50	John Knight,	private,	30
	51	Samuel Lacount,	do.	40

SCHEDULE OF PENSIONERS, continued.

District or Agency.	No. on the Roll.	NAMES.	Rank or Quality.	Annual Stipend.
New Hampshire,	52	Samuel Lathrop,	private,	60
	53	John Lapish,	do.	15
	54	Nathaniel Leavitt,	corporal,	60
	55	John Lincoln,	private,	36
	56	Joshua Lovejoy,	sergeant,	60
	57	Randall M'Allastar,	private,	60
	58	Andrew M'Gaffy,	lieutenant,	106 68
	59	John M'Coy,	private,	60
	60	Noah Marsh,	do.	20
	61	Joseph Morrell,	do.	60
	62	Jonathan Margery,	do.	40
	63	James Moore,	do.	60
	64	Samuel Morrell,	do.	24
	65	Joseph Moss,	do.	40
	66	Seymour Marsh,	do.	30
	67	Elijah Morse,	do.	48
	68	Jotham Nute,	sergeant,	60
	69	John Orr,	lieutenant,	120
	70	Phineas Parkhurst,	fifer,	60
	71	Joel Porter,	private,	15
	72	Samuel Potter,	sergeant,	40
	73	Asa Putney,	do.	30
	74	Jeremiah Pritchard,	lieutenant,	160
	75	Joseph Patterson,	private,	30
	76	Jonathan Perkins,	ensign,	60
	77	John Reed,	private,	60
	78	Stephen Richardson,	do.	24
	79	Daniel Russell,	do.	60
	80	Charles Rice,	do.	30
	81	Noah Robinson,	lieutenant,	120
	82	Joseph Richardson,	private,	30
	83	Joseph Slack,	do.	40
	84	John Samuel Sherburne,	major,	300
	85	Nathan Sanborn,	captain,	40
	86	Thomas Simpson,	lieutenant,	160
	87	Aaron Smith,	ensign,	120
	88	Noah Sinclair,	private,	45
	89	John Simpson,	do.	40
	90	Reuben Spencer,	do.	40
	91	John Smith,	sergeant,	30
	92	Samuel Stocker,	private,	30
	93	Amos Spafford,	do.	40
	94	Hezekiah Sawtell,	do.	30
	95	Samuel Sterns,	do.	30
	96	Jeremiah Towle,	corporal,	32
	97	Moses Trussell,	private,	40
	98	Ebenezer Tinkham,	do.	30
	99	William Taggart,	ensign,	60
	100	Nathan Taylor,	lieutenant,	120
	101	William Smart,	private,	60
	102	Jonathan Wilkins,	marine,	30
	103	William Wallace,	private,	60
	104	William Wood,	do.	40

SCHEDULE OF PENSIONERS, continued.

District or Agency.	No. on the Roll.	NAMES.	Rank or Quality.	Annual Stipend.	
New Hampshire,	105	Weymouth Wallace,	private,	30	
	106	Josiah Walton,	do.	20	
	107	Jacob Wilman, junior,	do.	15	
	108	Francis Whitcomb,	do.	20	
	109	Robert B. Wilkins,	do.	60	
	110	Seth Wyman,	do.	48	
	111	Edward Waldo,	lieutenant,	106	66⅔
	112	Jonathan Willard,	ensign,	60	
	113	Samuel Wells,	sergeant,	45	
	114	James Trowbridge,	do.	39	96
	115	Samuel Allen,	private,	24	
	116	Nehemiah Leavitt,	corporal,	30	
	117	William Powers,	private,	30	
	118	Lemuel Trafton, transferred from Massachusetts,	do.	60	
		Total of annual stipends,	. . . .	5,730	30½

SCHEDULE OF INVALID PENSIONERS, continued,

District or Agency.	No. on the Roll.	NAMES.	Rank or Quality.	Annual Stipend.
Massachusetts,	1	George Airs,	matross,	50
	2	Caleb Atherton,	private,	40
	3	John Adams,	do.	40
	4	Aaron Abbott,	do.	26 66
	5	Malachi Allen,	do.	20
	6	Luke Aldrich,	do.	30
	7	Gustavus Aldrich,	sergeant,	60
	8	Spafford Ames,	private,	60
	9	Robert Ames,	do.	60
	10	Isaac Abbot,	lieutenant,	96
	11	Ebenezer Bancroft,	captain,	72
	12	John Bryant,	lieutenant,	200
	13	Elias Barron,	dragoon,	60
	14	Joseph Brown,	sergeant,	60
	15	Jonathan Ball,	do.	48
	16	Perez Bradford,	do.	24
	17	Nathaniel Bowen,	do.	60
	18	John Barberie,	corporal,	60
	19	John Bean,	do.	40
	20	Benjamin Berry,	private,	60
	21	Abner Briggs,	do.	60
	22	Phineas Butler,	do.	60
	23	Peter Barrows,	do.	28
	24	Jonas Blodget,	do.	40
	25	Nathaniel Baker,	do.	40
	26	Squire Bishop, junior,	do.	40
	27	Josiah Ball,	do.	26 66
	28	George Bacon,	do.	48
	29	Ephraim Bailey,	do.	60
	30	Robert Bancroft,	do.	10
	31	James Bacheldore,	do.	15
	32	John Berry,	do.	60
	33	Elijah Brainard,	do.	60
	34	Ebenezer Brown,	sergeant,	60
	35	Joshua Clapp,	lieutenant,	(dead)
	36	Josiah Chute,	sergeant,	40
	37	Abel Carpenter,	do.	26 66
	38	Jonas Childs,	private,	60
	39	Job Carwell,	do.	60
	40	Timothy Chase,	do.	40
	41	William Conant,	do.	40
	42	Moses Cass,	do.	40
	43	Levi Chadbourne,	do.	60
	44	Solomon Cole,	do.	26 66
	45	Noah Clough,	do.	15
	46	Nathan Cook,	do.	14
	47	Richard Crouch,	do.	60
	48	James Campbel,	do.	15
	49	Caleb Chadwick,	do.	15
	50	Barnabas Chapman,	do.	20
	51	Richard Chase,	do.	30
	52	Joseph Coxe,	sergeant,	40
	53	Thomas Crowell,	private,	60

SCHEDULE OF PENSIONERS, continued.

District or Agency.	No. on the Roll.	NAMES.	Rank or Quality.	Annual Stipend.
Massachusetts,	54	George Cammell,	private,	$ 30
	55	John Careton,	do.	30
	56	Henry Carver,	do.	60
	57	William Clark,	do.	30
	58	Seth Delana,	sergeant,	32
	59	Thomas Doty,	private,	60
	60	Jonathan Davis,	do.	30
	61	John Duncan,	do.	26 66
	62	Jonathan Doty,	marine,	33 32
	63	Robert Elvell,	bombardier,	60
	64	William Earle,	marine,	60
	65	John Elgerly,	private,	60
	66	Henry Farwell,	captain,	80
	67	Jonas Farnsworth,	do.	120
	68	John Francis,	do.	60
	69	William Foster,	sergeant,	48
	70	Samuel Fowle,	private,	40
	71	Jedediah Fuller,	do.	40
	72	Jacob Frost,	do.	30
	73	Levi Farnsworth,	do.	30
	74	Moses Fitch,	do.	12
	75	Frederick Follet,	do.	30
	76	Joseph Frost,	do.	7 50
	77	Benjamin Farnham,	captain,	80
	78	Thomas Foot,	private,	40
	79	John Gould,	do.	60
	80	Jonathan Gleason,	do.	60
	81	Silas Gill,	do.	40
	82	Samuel Green,	do.	20
	83	Isaac Greer,	do.	10
	84	Henry Gates,	do.	60
	85	Uriah Goodwin,	do.	15
	86	Deborah Gannett,	do.	48
	87	Charles Gowen,	do.	30
	88	Edward Grant,	do.	44 40
	89	Elijah Hudson,	sergeant,	48
	90	Solomon Hayward,	do.	48
	91	Daniel Horn,	do.	20
	92	John Hicks,	private,	60
	93	Daniel Hickey,	do.	60
	94	Peter Hopkins,	do.	40
	95	Joseph Handy,	do.	30
	96	Josiah Howard,	do.	26 66
	97	Daniel Hemmenway,	do.	20
	98	William Hubbard,	marine,	60
	99	Joseph Hale,	private,	(dead.)
	100	Gamaliel Handy,	do.	40
	101	Peter Hemmenway,	do.	60
	102	Jesse Holt,	corporal,	7 50
	103	Ambrose Homan,	private,	30

SCHEDULE OF PENSIONERS, continued.

District or Agency.	No. on the Roll.	NAMES.	Rank or Quality.	Annual Stipend.
Massachusetts,	104	William Jacobs,	private,	60
	105	Joseph Johnson,	do.	60
	106	Josiah Jones,	do.	48
	107	Moses Knowland,	do.	60
	108	Abner Kent,	do.	60
	109	John Knowles,	do.	20
	110	Ephraim Lane,	Lt. colonel,	20
	111	Thomas Linnen,	corporal,	20
	112	William Lucas,	private,	60
	113	Crosby Luce,	gunner,	30
	114	Nathaniel Ladd,	private,	30
	115	Reuben Mitchell,	do.	60
	116	Neil M'Arthur,	do.	60
	117	Isaac M'Kinney,	do.	40
	118	Benjamin Moody,	do.	40
	119	Benjamin Mastick,	do.	60
	120	Alexander Murray,	do.	30
	121	Benjamin Merrill,	do.	40
	122	Filley Mead,	do.	15
	123	Elisha Munsell,	do.	30
	124	John Maynard,	lieutenant,	72
	125	Samuel Mears, junior,	private,	30
	126	Christopher, Newbitt,	do.	60
	127	John Nickless,	do.	10
	128	Daniel Nutting,	do.	24
	129	Timothy Northam,	do.	20
	130	Joseph Noyes,	lieutenant,	30
	131	John Paul,	sergeant,	48
	132	Joseph Patterson,	do.	30
	133	George Parker,	private,	48
	134	Solomon Parsons,	do.	48
	135	John Priest,	do.	40
	136	Nathan Putnam,	do.	5
	137	Ebenezer Perkins,	marine,	60
	138	William Parker,	private,	30
	139	Joseph Peabody,	do.	20
	140	Amos Peirson,	sergeant,	12
	141	Job Preist,	ensign,	40
	142	Thomas Pratt,	private,	40
	143	Jonathan Patch,	do.	60
	144	Shephard Packard,	do.	36
	145	Joseph Roberts,	carpenter,	60
	146	Elisha Rice,	corporal,	60
	147	Abner Rose,	matross,	33 32
	148	Moses Ramsdale,	private,	60
	149	Benjamin Rider,	do.	60
	150	Eliphas Reed,	do.	60
	151	Benjamin A. Richardson,	do.	40
	152	William Rideout,	do.	60
	153	Jeremiah Robbins,	do.	40
	154	Joseph Rumrill,	do.	40

SCHEDULE OF PENSIONERS, continued.

District or Agency.	No. on the Roll.	NAMES.	Rank or Quality.	Annual Stipend.
Massachusetts,	155	Ebenezer Rowe,	seaman,	$ 60
	156	John Slewman,	captain,	300
	157	Eli Stearns,	sergeant,	60
	158	Ezekiel Spalding,	do.	24
	159	Joseph Saunders,	corporal,	60
	160	Jonathan Stevens,	do.	30
	161	John Stoak,	private,	60
	162	Anthony Shoppe,	do.	60
	163	Jonas Shattuck,	do.	60
	164	Zenas Sturdivant,	do.	60
	165	Moses Smith,	do.	60
	166	Enoch Stocker,	do.	40
	167	Anthony Starbard,	do.	40
	168	William Symms,	do.	37 50
	169	Daniel Stearns,	do.	36
	170	Abraham Sawyer,	do.	30
	171	William Spooner,	bombardier,	(dead.)
	172	Amasa Scott,	private,	15
	173	Robert Smith,	do.	40
	174	Sylvanus Snow,	do.	20
	175	Abner Snow,	do.	45
	176	Moses Sanderson,	do.	40
	177	Peleg Smith,	do.	40
	178	Jonathan Taft,	do.	60
	179	Lemuel Trafton,	do.	transferred.
	180	Israel Thomas,	do.	60
	181	Noah Taylor,	do.	60
	182	Ephraim Taylor,	do.	60
	183	Charles Thrasher,	do.	40
	184	John Tolman,	do.	transferred.
	185	Peleg Tallman,	yeoman,	51
	186	Philip Taber,	private,	60
	187	Eliphalet Taylor,	private,	20
	188	Josiah Temple,	do.	40
	189	George Ulmer,	lieutenant,	160
	190	John Union,	private,	30
	191	Amariah Vose,	sergeant,	60
	192	David Vickery,	private,	20
	193	Moses White,	captain,	240
	194	James Warner,	lieutenant,	120
	195	Joseph Whittemore,	do.	120
	196	David Wood,	sergeant,	48
	197	Elijah Williams,	corporal,	60
	198	William Watts,	private,	60
	199	Isaac Whitcomb,	do.	(dead.)
	200	Joshua Winn,	do.	48
	201	Joseph Ware,	do.	60
	202	Asa Ware,	do.	60
	203	Josiah Wright,	do.	48

SCHEDULE OF PENSIONERS, continued.

District or Agency.	No. on the Roll.	NAMES.	Rank or Quality.	Annual Stipend.
Massachusetts,	204	Elisha Ward,	private,	40
	205	Samuel Woodbury,	marine,	40
	206	Wareham Warner,	private,	36
	207	Moses Wing,	drummer,	60
	208	Samuel Warner,	private,	30
	209	Samuel Willington,	do.	30
	210	Nahum Wright,	sergeant,	7 50
	211	William Warren,	lieutenant,	90
	212	James Wesson,	colonel,	300
	213	William Cushing,	lieutenant,	120
	214	Wm. Leaver, alias Lavar,	private,	30
	215	Oliver Russell,	corporal,	30
	216	James Walsh,	matross,	60
	217	Jas. Gallute, transf. fr. N. Y.	private,	36
				10,602 33

SCHEDULE OF PENSIONERS, continued.

District or Agency.	No on the Roll.	NAMES.	Rank or Quality.	Annual Stipend.
Vermont,	1	Jonas Adams,	private,	$ 60
	2	William Beden,	corporal,	36
	3	Samuel Bradish,	private,	60
	4	Daniel Brown,	do.	60
	5	Elijah Barnes,	do.	15
	6	Elijah Bennett,	do.	30
	7	Thomas Brush,	do.	15
	8	David Brydia,	do.	30
	9	Joseph Bird,	do.	48
	10	Daniel Cushman,	corporal,	(transf.)
	11	Gershom Clark,	private,	60
	12	James Campbell,	do.	30
	13	Edward Clark,	sergeant,	15
	14	Elisha Capron,	private,	30
	15	Oliver Darling,	do.	60
	16	Samuel Eyers,	do.	60
	17	Richard Fairbrother,	do.	36
	18	Thomas Green,	do.	40
	19	Asa Gould,	do.	60
	20	Benjamin Gould,	do.	50
	21	Amasa Grover,	do.	24
	22	Ezra Gates,	do.	40
	23	Gideon Griggs,	do.	30
	24	William Hazletine,	do.	60
	25	Jediah Hyde,	captain,	180
	26	Jonathan Haynes,	private,	40
	27	Zimri Hill,	do.	30
	28	Lewis Hurd,	sergeant,	60
	29	Joseph Huntoon,	lieutenant,	160
	30	Jared Hinckley, junior,	private,	30
	31	Nathan Jaques,	do.	20
	32	Elijah Knight,	do.	60
	33	Jonathan Lake,	corporal,	30
	34	Jonathan Lyon,	private,	60
	35	Eleazer Martin,	do.	40
	36	Ebenezer M'Ilvaine,	do.	60
	37	William Martin,	do.	40
	38	Richard Millen,	do.	60
	39	John Nixon,	colonel,	150
	40	Nehemiah Peirce,	private,	60
	41	Elisha Reynolds,	do.	30
	42	Prince Robinson,	do.	60
	43	Uriah Stone,	steward,	60
	44	Daniel Stanton, junior,	private,	45
	45	Ephraim Smith,	do.	60
	46	Philo Stoddard,	do.	40
	47	Thomas Torrance,	do.	30
	48	Benjamin Tower,	do.	40
	49	Joseph Tyler,	do.	60
	50	Annanias Tubbs,	do.	30

SCHEDULE OF PENSIONERS, continued.

District or Agency.	No. on the Roll.	NAMES.	Rank or Quality.	Annual Stipend.
Vermont, .	51	Abel Woods,	private,	$ 60
	52	Aaron Wilder,	do.	60
	53	Jonathan Woolley,	do.	60
	54	Ziba Woodworth,	do.	60
	55	William Waterman,	do.	20
	56	John Wilson,	sergeant,	20
	57	Isaac Webster,	do.	30
	58	Daniel Evans,	private,	30
	59	Nathan Ford,	do.	30
	60	Jonas Hobart,	do.	24
	61	Lemuel Rich, (from Con.)	do.	60
	62	John Tolman, (from Mass.)	do.	20
		Total of annual stipends,	. . . .	2,938

SCHEDULE OF PENSIONERS, continued.

District or Agency.	No. on the Roll.	NAMES.	Rank or Quality.	Annual Stipend.
Rhode Island, .	1	Thomas Arnold,	captain,	$ 240
	2	Abijah Adams,	private,	54
	3	John Armsbury,	do.	30
	4	William Barton,	sergeant,	42
	5	Edward Bennett,	private,	60
	6	Comfort Bishop,	do.	40
	7	Jacob Briggs,	do.	48
	8	George Bradford,	do.	60
	9	Ezra Chase,	do.	60
	10	James Chappel,	do.	42
	11	Levi Cæsar,	do.	36
	12	Rowland Chadsey,	do.	20
	13	Jonathan Davenport,	do.	2 50
	14	Comfort Eddy,	do.	60
	15	John Elloit,	do.	30
	16	Edward Gavett,	do.	60
	17	Job Greenman,	do.	48
	18	Prince Green,	do.	48
	19	Richard Hopkins,	do.	30
	20	Josiah Jones,	do.	60
	21	William Lunt,	do.	30
	22	John Mowry,	do.	27
	23	Edward Peirce,	sergeant,	60
	24	Bristol Rhodes,	private,	60
	25	Joseph A Richards,	corporal,	42
	26	John Slocum,	private,	60
	27	Richard Sephton,	do.	60
	28	Britain Saltonstall,	do.	42
	29	Charles Scott,	do.	60
	30	Benoni Simmons,	gunner,	60
	31	Noel Tabor,	corporal,	27
	32	Benjamin Tompkins,	marine,	60
	33	George Townsend,	private,	45
	34	Prince Vaughan,	do.	44
	35	Edward Vose,	sergeant,	10
	36	Guy Watson,	private,	30
		Total of annual stipends,	. . . .	1,787 50

SCHEDULE OF PENSIONERS, continued.

District or Agency.	No. on the Roll.	NAMES.	Rank or Quality.	Annual Stipend.
Connecticut,	1	Thomas Avery,	lieutenant,	8 200
	2	Park Avery, junior,	do.	60
	3	Ebenezer Avery,	corporal,	30
	4	David Atkins,	private,	60
	5	Gad Asher,	do.	60
	6	Abner Andruss,	do.	60
	7	Daniel Avery,	do.	36
	8	Amos Avery, 2d,	do.	30
	9	Theodore Andruss,	do.	60
	10	Samuel Andruss,	corporal,	45
	11	Smith Ames,	private,	60
	12	Nathaniel Austin,	do.	45
	13	Daniel Bouton,	captain,	180
	14	Oliver Bostwick,	ensign,	120
	15	Daniel Bushnell,	private,	60
	16	Simeon Bishop,	do.	60
	17	Salmon Buell,	do.	(dead)
	18	William Burrows,	do.	60
	19	Daniel Bill,	do.	60
	20	Isaiah Bunce,	do.	45
	21	Stephen Barnum,	do.	60
	22	Samuel Burdwin,	do.	60
	23	Benjamin Bennett,	do.	24
	24	John Beardsley, junior,	do.	60
	25	Jedediah Brown,	do.	20
	26	Elisha Burrows,	do.	15
	27	Isaiah Beaumont,	do.	15
	28	Walter Burdick,	do.	30
	29	Edward Bassett,	do.	30
	30	William Bailey,	do.	30
	31	Robert Bailey,	do.	15
	32	Enos Blakesley,	do.	(dead.)
	33	David Blackman,	do.	40
	34	Jonathan Bowers,	corporal,	60
	35	Aner Bradley,	sergeant,	30
	36	Oliver Burnham,	do.	15
	37	Isaiah Buell,	private,	45
	38	Joseph Button,	do.	60
	39	Seth Boardman,	do.	40
	40	William C. Bebee,	do.	60
	41	Ebenezer Coe,	captain,	240
	42	Richard Chamberlain,	private,	44
	43	John Clark,	do.	60
	44	Matthew Cadwell,	do.	60
	45	Benoni Connell,	do.	60
	46	Jirah Carter,	do.	60
	47	Timothy Ceasar,	do.	60
	48	Benjamin Close,	do.	48
	49	Amariah Chappell,	do.	24
	50	Elisha Clark,	do.	30
	51	Jonah Cook,	do.	60
	52	Henry Cone,	do.	60
	53	Simon Crosby,	do.	40

SCHEDULE OF PENSIONERS, continued.

District or Agency.	No. on the Roll.	NAMES.	Rank or Quality.	Annual Stipend.
Connecticut,	54	Nathaniel Church,	private,	30
	55	Ebenezer Duran,	do.	60
	56	George Dixon,	do.	60
	57	Lemuel Denning, junior,	do.	20
	58	Lothrop Davis,	sergeant,	60
	59	Israel Dibble,	private,	36
	60	Gershom Dormon,	do.	60
	61	Joseph Dunbar,	corporal,	45
	62	John Daboll,	private,	7 50
	63	Stephen Everts,	do.	40
	64	William Edmonds,	do.	40
	65	Eliphalet Easton,	do.	60
	66	Gideon Edwards,	do.	60
	67	Stephen Fellows,	sergeant,	60
	68	Thomas Farnham,	do.	36
	69	John Fountaine,	private,	60
	70	Aaron Farmar,	do.	60
	71	Isaac Frink,	do.	60
	72	Ransford A. Ferris,	do.	60
	73	Zaccheus Fargo,	do.	30
	74	Henry Filmore,	do.	30
	75	Samuel French,	do.	60
	76	Andrew Griswold,	lieutenant,	160
	77	Sherman Gardner,	private,	60
	78	Henry Gilner,	do.	60
	79	Andrew Gallup,	do.	40
	80	Robert Gallup,	do.	15
	81	Richard P. Hallow,	do.	60
	82	Jazaniah How,	do.	60
	83	Stephen Hull,	corporal,	30
	84	Joseph Harrup,	private,	60
	85	Stephen Hempstead,	do.	45
	86	Nero Hawley,	do.	40
	87	Isee Hayt,	do.	30
	88	John Herron,	do.	30
	89	Eleazer Hudson,	do.	45
	90	Ashbel Hosmer,	corporal,	(dead)
	91	Nathan Hawley,	do.	48
	92	Daniel Hewitt,	sergeant,	20
	93	Isaac Higgins,	private,	(dead)
	94	Thurston Hilliard,	do.	20
	95	John Horsford,	do.	(dead)
	96	Benjamin Howd,	do.	45
	97	Elijah Hoyt,	do.	30
	98	David Hubbell,	do.	60
	99	Nathaniel Hewitt,	do.	45
	100	Joel Hinman,	do.	60
	101	David Hurd,	do.	60
	102	Charles Jones,	do.	60
	103	Justus Johnson,	do.	40
	104	Johuel Judd,	do.	48
	105	Lent Ives,	do.	30
	106	Caleb Jewett,	do.	20

SCHEDULE OF PENSIONERS, continued.

District or Agency.	No. on the Roll.	NAMES.	Rank or Quality.	Annual Stipend.
Connecticut,	107	William Johnson,	private,	30
	108	Jared Knapp,	sergeant,	60
	109	Lemuel King,	private,	60
	110	Elisha Lee,	captain,	240
	111	Peter Lewis,	private,	60
	112	Phineas Lake,	do.	60
	113	William Leach,	do.	60
	114	Christopher Latham, junior,	do.	45
	115	John Ledyard,	do.	45
	116	Naboth Lewis,	do.	40
	117	Nathaniel Lewis,	do.	15
	118	Samuel Loomis,	corporal,	45
	119	Lee Lay,	captain,	80
	120	Elijah Lincoln,	corporal,	60
	121	Timothy Mix,	lieutenant,	60
	122	Andrew Mead,	ensign,	80
	123	Dan Mansfield,	private,	(dead)
	124	Samuel Mitchell,	do.	60
	125	Samuel Mills, junior,	do.	30
	126	John Morgan, 3d,	do.	40
	127	Jacob Meach,	do.	20
	128	James Morgan, junior,	do.	30
	129	Joseph Moxley,	do.	30
	130	Jeremiah Markham,	sergeant,	60
	131	Allyn Marsh,	corporal,	30
	132	Stephen Miner,	qr. gunner,	30
	133	Elnathan Norton,	private,	(dead)
	134	Mark Noble,	do.	60
	135	David Orcutt,	do.	60
	136	Joseph Otis,	do.	30
	137	Thomas Picket,	do.	60
	138	Alexander Phelps,	do.	60
	139	David Pool,	do.	60
	140	Thomas Parmelie,	sergeant,	7 50
	141	Chandler Pardie,	private,	52 50
	142	Daniel Preston,	do.	20
	143	Obadiah Perkins,	lieutenant,	96
	144	Enos Petott,	private,	24
	145	John Rood,	do.	48
	146	Jeremiah Ryan,	do.	60
	147	Lemuel Rich,	do.	(transfd.)
	148	Moses Raymond,	do.	60
	149	Oliver Rogers,	do.	24
	150	David Ranney,	do.	60
	151	Solomon Reynolds,	do.	60
	152	Samuel Rossetter,	do.	60
	153	Elijah Royce,	do.	45
	154	Josiah Smith,	do.	60
	155	Edward Stanton,	do.	60
	156	Josiah Strong,	do.	40
	157	John Starr,	do.	40
	158	Selah Schoffield,	do.	30
	159	William Seymour,	do.	240

SCHEDULE OF PENSIONERS, continued.

District or Agency.	No. on the Roll.	NAMES.	Rank or Quality.	Annual Stipend.
Connecticut, .	160	Benjamin Seely,	private,	15
	161	William Starr,	qr. master,	45
	162	Elihu Sabin,	private,	40
	163	Samuel Sawyer,	do.	30
	164	Thomas Shepherd,	do.	15
	165	Amos Skeel,	do.	60
	166	Heber Smith,	sergeant,	60
	167	Aaron Smith,	private,	15
	168	Edmund Smith,	do.	30
	169	Samuel Stillman,	do.	30
	170	Aaron Stephens,	captain,	120
	171	Peter Smith,	private,	48
	172	Elijah Sheldon,	do.	(dead)
	173	John Smith,	do.	48
	174	Moses Tracy,	sergeant,	60
	175	William Tarball,	corporal,	36
	176	Solomon Townsend,	private,	60
	177	Aaron Tuttle,	do.	40
	178	Jabez Tomlinson,	do.	15
	179	Enoch Turner, junior,	do.	60
	180	Levi Tuttle,	do.	15
	181	Samuel Woodcock.	sergeant,	60
	182	Constant Webb,	do.	36
	183	William Wilson,	private,	60
	184	John Waklee,	do.	60
	185	Joseph Waterman,	do.	40
	186	Benjamin Weed, junior,	do.	30
	187	Joseph Woodmansee,	do.	60
	188	Thomas Williams,	do.	20
	189	Jacob Williams,	do.	15
	190	Richard Watrous,	do.	45
	191	Jonathan Whaley,	do.	15
	192	Ezra Wilcox,	do.	15
	193	Azel Woodworth,	do.	60
	194	Seth Weed,	lieutenant,	72
	195	James Wayland,	private,	40
	196	William Woodruff,	corporal,	60
	197	Hezekiah Bailey,	ensign,	60
	198	Isaac Durand,	private,	30
	199	Joel Fox,	do.	30
	200	Luke Guyant,	do.	60
	201	Aaron Peck,	do.	40
		Total of annual stipends,	. . . .	9,778 50

SCHEDULE OF PENSIONERS, continued.

District or Agency.	No. on the Roll.	NAMES.	Rank or Quality.	Annual Stipend.
New York,	1	James Adams,	sergeant,	$ 60
	2	Matthew Adams,	private,	60
	3	Gannett Abeel,	do.	48
	4	Edward Armstrong,	do.	36
	5	Jacob Acker,	do.	36
	6	Richard Allison,	do.	24
	7	Waterman Baldwin,	do.	60
	8	Joshua Barnum,	captain,	240
	9	Nathan Bradley,	private,	60
	10	Henry Brewster,	lieutenant,	120
	11	David Brown,	do.	96
	12	Nicholas Barrett *alias* Barth,	do.	135
	13	Thomas Boyce,	ensign,	96
	14	James Burgess,	qr. mr. sergt	24
	15	Silas Barber,	sergeant,	60
	16	Jonas Belknap,	do.	20
	17	Joshua Bishop,	matross,	36
	18	John Bennett,	private,	60
	19	John Butler,	do.	60
	20	Timothy Bowen,	do.	60
	21	Nicholas Bovie,	do.	60
	22	Edward Benton,	do.	60
	23	Henry Bouce,	do.	60
	24	John Baxter,	do.	48
	25	John Brooks,	do.	36
	26	Obadiah Banks,	do.	36
	27	George H. Bell,	do.	30
	28	Michael Brooks,	do.	24
	29	Nicholas Brown,	do.	24
	30	Baltus Bradenburgh,	do.	24
	31	Edward Bates,	do.	60
	32	Thomas Baldwin,	sergeant,	30
	33	Thomas Brooks,	private,	45
	34	Jedediah Brown,	do.	30
	35	William Burritt,	do	60
	36	Job Bartram,	captain,	180
	37	Caleb Brewster,	lieutenant,	200
	38	Obadiah Brown,	private,	15
	39	Benjamin Benjamin,	do.	60
	40	James Beers,	do	48
	41	Benjamin Bartlett,	sergeant,	60
	42	Daniel Baldwin,	captain,	240
	43	Aaron Brink,	private,	60
	44	Peter Covenhoven,	sergeant,	60
	45	David Cook,	captain,	200
	46	Thomas Carpenter,	lieutenant,	96
	47	Joseph Cutler,	ensign,	60
	48	Philo Carfield,	sergeant,	24
	49	Thomas Crawford,	bombardier,	60
	50	Edward Callaghan,	private,	60
	51	John Cooper,	do.	60
	52	Gershom Curvin,	do.	60
	53	Adam Coppernoll,	do.	60

SCHEDULE OF PENSIONERS, continued.

District or Agency.	No. on the Roll.	NAMES.	Rank or Quality.	Annual Stipend.
New York,	54	David Cady,	private,	$ 60
	55	Daniel Culver,	do.	60
	56	Amos Camp,	do.	40
	57	Francis Courtney,	do.	40
	58	Gilbert Carrigan,	do.	36
	59	John Crum,	do.	36
	60	Phineas Coxe,	do.	30
	61	William Champernois,	do.	45
	62	Russell Chappell,	do.	30
	63	Henry Challer,	do.	60
	64	Aaron Crane,	sergeant,	30
	65	Albert Chapman,	captain,	120
	66	John Cramer,	private,	30
	67	Peter Conyne,	adjutant,	96
	68	Hackaliah Doolittle,	private,	30
	69	Hans Mark Demoth,	captain,	240
	70	Francis Delong,	lieutenant,	60
	71	Andrew Dunlop,	sergeant,	60
	72	Thomas Duncan,	do.	60
	73	William Drew,	corporal,	36
	74	Nathan Davis,	private,	60
	75	James Dunlap,	do.	60
	76	Mathias Decamp,	do.	60
	77	George Dunkill,	do.	60
	78	Samuel Decker,	do.	60
	79	Marshal Dixon,	do.	24
	80	Thomas Done,	matross,	60
	81	James Dole,	lieutenant,	100
	82	Peter Demarest,	private,	60
	83	John De Voe,	do.	60
	84	Benjamin Denslow,	do.	60
	85	Gerardus Dingman,	do.	60
	86	Jared Duncan,	do.	60
	87	Isaac Elwood,	corporal,	48
	88	Nathan Ellis,	private,	60
	89	William Elberton,	do.	60
	90	Jeremiah Everitt,	do.	30
	91	Peter Eager,	do.	60
	92	Frederick Fisher,	colonel,	300
	93	John Frey,	brigade major,	300
	94	Christian W. Fox,	captain,	240
	95	William Faulkner,	do.	90
	96	Hackaliah Foster,	sergeant,	30
	97	Robert Feeks,	corporal,	48
	98	Squire Fancher,	private,	60
	99	William Fagan,	do.	60
	100	Duncan Frazier,	do.	60
	101	John Foster,	do.	60
	102	Andrew Frank,	do.	60
	103	John Jost Foltz,	do.	60

SCHEDULE OF PENSIONERS, continued.

District. or Agency.	No. on the Roll.	NAMES.	Rank or Quality.	Annual Stipend.
New York.	104	Jonathan Finch,	private,	$ 48
	105	George Finchley,	do.	48
	106	Sylvanus Ferris,	do.	36
	107	Elisha Frizzle,	do.	60
	108	William Fancher,	do.	24
	109	John Ferris,	do.	24
	110	Elisha Farnham,	do.	30
	111	Elisha Forbes,	do.	36
	112	John Fleming,	do.	60
	113	William Foster,	do.	60
	114	Richard Garrison,	qr. master,	78
	115	Jacob Gardiner,	captain,	120
	116	Nathaniel Gove,	lieutenant,	160
	117	Samuel Gibbs,	do.	160
	118	Zachariah Green,	corporal,	36
	119	John Garnett,	private,	60
	120	Samuel Gardiner,	do.	60
	121	Josiah Green,	do.	48
	122	James Gallute,	do.	(transf.)
	123	Benajah Geer,	do.	24
	124	Allen Gilbert,	do.	15
	125	Isaac Genung,	do.	30
	126	Francis Gallaher,	do.	60
	127	Burr Gilbert,	do.	60
	128	Simeon Gibbs,	corporal,	30
	129	John Gilbert,	sergeant,	30
	130	Thomas Hustler,	do.	60
	131	David Hall, junior,	do.	60
	132	George Helmer,	lieutenant,	156
	133	Mordecai Hall,	sugeons mate,	189
	134	Staats Hammond,	sergeant,	60
	135	John Hilton,	do.	24
	136	Stephen Hurlbut,	drummer,	48
	137	John Hink,	private,	60
	138	Joseph Harris,	do.	60
	139	Thomas Hinds,	do.	60
	140	Adam Hartman,	do.	52
	141	George Hansel,	do.	48
	142	Peter Hogaboom,	do.	40
	143	Thomas Hill,	do.	30
	144	Asa Hill,	do.	24
	145	Ozias Handford.	do.	24
	146	Joseph Hager,	do.	15
	147	Henry Hopper,	do.	12
	148	John Hess,	do.	12
	149	Bartlett Hinds,	lieutenant,	80
	150	John Hubbard,	private,	36
	151	Humphrey Hunt,	do.	15
	152	Charlotte Hazen,	. . . .	200
	153	Joseph Harker,	captain,	120

SCHEDULE OF PENSIONERS, continued.

District or Agency.	No. on the Roll.	NAMES.	Rank or Quality.	Annual Stipend.
New York,	154	Peter Harford,	sergeant,	$ 30
	155	David Hamilton,	private,	60
	156	Samuel Jones,	sergeant,	60
	157	James Ivory,	private,	60
	158	William Jump,	do.	24
	159	William James,	do.	24
	160	Elijah Janes,	do.	100
	161	Leverinus Koch,	sergeant,	60
	162	Johannes Koch.	do.	36
	163	Reuben King,	private,	60
	164	John Kalb,	do.	60
	165	Joseph Knapp,	do.	48
	166	Feorge Knox,	do.	36
	167	John Ketchum,	do.	36
	168	Abiel Knapp,	do.	40
	169	John King,	do.	45
	170	Elijah Knapp,	sergeant,	30
	171	Stephen Kellog,	private,	60
	172	Thomas Lyon,	lieutenant,	120
	173	Henry Lewis,	ensign,	30
	174	Robert Lang,	sergeant,	48
	175	Moses Lockwood,	gunner,	36
	176	William Lewis,	private,	36
	177	Michael Lyons,	do.	48
	178	Peter Lampman,	do.	48
	179	William Laken,	do.	40
	180	John Little,	captain,	240
	181	Joseph M'Craken,	major,	300
	182	John M'Kinstry,	captain,	240
	183	Michael Myers,	sergeant,	60
	184	Lilleus Mead,	do.	60
	185	Alexander M'Nish,	do.	52
	186	Amos Miner,	do.	30
	187	Mead Marshall,	gunner,	60
	188	John Millspaugh,	bombardier,	36
	189	Alexander M'Coy,	do.	24
	190	George Mour,	private,	60
	191	Charles M'Kenny,	do.	60
	192	Girardus Mook,	do.	60
	193	John M'Intosh,	do.	60
	194	Daniel M'Donald,	do.	48
	195	Paul M'Fall,	do.	48
	196	John Mosher,	do.	48
	197	Samuel M'Kean,	do.	36
	198	William Martine,	do.	36
	199	Philip Martine,	do.	36
	200	John Miller,	co.	30
	201	Henry Murphey,	do.	24
	202	Daniel Mowris,	do.	24
	203	Hugh M'Master,	do.	12
	204	Francis Monty,	lieutenant,	80
	205	Samuel Miller,	private,	60
	206	Michael Malony,	do.	60

SCHEDULE OF PENSIONERS, continued.

District or Agency.	No. on the Roll.	NAMES.	Rank or Quality.	Annual Stipend.
New York,	207	Thomas Machin,	captain,	$ 120
	208	Joseph Mack,	private,	24
	209	Thomas M'Grath,	do.	30
	210	William M'Laland,	do.	60
	211	Donald M'Donald,	hostler,	30
	212	Abraham Nealy,	lieutenant,	120
	213	Jacob Newkirk,	private,	36
	214	David Nicholls,	corporal,	48
	215	Garret Oblenis,	private,	30
	216	James Philips,	do.	30
	217	Joseph Prenhop,	lieutenant,	80
	218	Solomon Purdy,	sergeant,	60
	219	Joseph Passmore,	do.	60
	220	Jonathan Purdy,	corporal,	60
	221	Thomas Powell,	private,	60
	222	Daniel Provost,	do.	60
	223	Stephen Plumb,	do.	36
	224	Silas Parish,	do.	36
	225	Adolph Picard,	do.	30
	226	Garret Peck,	do.	24
	227	Jared Palmer,	sergeant,	30
	228	Stephen Powell,	private,	3 75
	229	Joel Phelps,	do.	30
	230	Abner Pier,	do.	30
	231	Jonathan Pollard,	do.	60
	232	William Patterson,	do.	60
	233	Elisha Prior,	do.	45
	234	David Pendleton,	do.	60
	235	John Quick,	do.	24
	236	Philip Philips,	do.	30
	237	Nicholas Ritcher,	captain,	240
	238	John Requa,	private,	60
	239	Israel Reeves,	do.	60
	240	Robert Robertson,	do.	60
	241	Jacob Rattenauer,	do.	60
	242	Jonathan Reynolds,	do.	(dead.)
	243	John Rice,	do.	48
	244	Joseph Rehern,	do.	42
	245	Hendrick Ritchmeyer,	do.	42
	246	William Reynolds,	do.	40
	247	Frederick Rasberg,	do.	24
	248	John Renan,	do.	12
	249	Isaac Richards,	do.	30
	250	John Rogers,	do.	30
	251	James Reeves,	do.	36
	252	Benjamin Reynolds,	do.	24
	253	John St. John,	do.	60
	254	Samuel Shaw,	lieutenant,	96
	255	William Scott,	major,	300
	256	Philip Staats,	lieutenant,	96
	257	Josiah Smith,	do.	120
	258	James Stilwell,	sergeant,	60
	259	William Sloan,	do.	40

SCHEDULE OF PENSIONERS, continued.

District or Agency.	No. on the Roll.	NAMES.	Rank or Quality.	Annual Stipend.
New York,	260	John Stewart,	corporal,	$ 48
	261	James Sartine,	private,	60
	262	Daniel Stevens,	do.	60
	263	Pearl Sharks,	do.	60
	264	Robert Saunders,	do.	60
	265	John Shutliff,	do.	60
	266	Sylvanus Seely,	do.	48
	267	Cornelius Swartwout,	do.	48
	268	James Scott,	do.	48
	269	Henry Seeber,	do.	48
	270	Abiel Sherman,	do.	36
	271	Benjamin Smith,	do.	60
	272	James Smith,	do.	36
	273	George Stansel,	do.	36
	274	Garret Sulback,	do.	36
	275	Adam Stroback,	do.	36
	276	Edward Scott,	do.	36
	277	James Slater,	do.	30
	278	Thaddeus Seeley,	do.	30
	279	Hans Jost Snell,	do.	24
	280	George Schell,	do.	60
	281	Finley Stewart,	batteau man,	45
	282	Godfrey Sweet,	private,	60
	283	John Shay,	do.	36
	284	Eliphalet Sherwood,	do.	30
	285	Benjamin Sturges,	do.	48
	286	Silas Talbot,	lt. colonel,	300
	287	Jacob Traviss,	lieutenant,	160
	288	John Thomas,	private,	60
	289	Ezekiel Travis,	do.	48
	290	Ebenezer Tyler,	do.	48
	291	Daniel Townsend,	do.	40
	292	Willam Tanner,	do.	32
	293	Asa Taylor,	do.	30
	294	John Taylor,	do.	36
	295	Alexander Tilford,	do.	24
	296	Henry Ten Eyck,	captain,	180
	297	Abel Turney,	marine,	60
	298	Daniel Treadwell,	private,	48
	299	Henry C. Van Ransalaer,	lieut. colonel,	360
	300	William Van Ward,	private,	36
	301	John Utters, .	do.	60
	302	John Vaughn,	sergeant,	15
	303	Asa Virgil,	private,	15
	304	John Venus,	do.	30
	305	Isaac Vincent,	do.	60
	306	William Wallace,	lieutenant,	96
	307	James Wier,	corporal,	52
	308	David Wendell,	private,	60
	309	Thomas Ward,	do.	60
	310	George Waggoner,	do.	60

SCHEDULE OF PENSIONERS, continued.

District or Agency.	No. on the Roll.	NAMES.	Rank or Quality.	Annual Stipend.
New York, .	311	Jacob Wright,	private,	$ 60
	312	Thomas Wilson,	do.	60
	313	Abraham Wolhlever,	do.	60
	314	David Wilson,	do.	48
	315	John Winn,	do.	48
	316	Lemuel Wood,	do.	36
	317	Nicholas Walrath,	do.	36
	318	William White,	do.	40
	319	James Wills,	do.	30
	320	Ichabod Williams,	do.	24
	321	Isaiah Wright,	do.	24
	322	David Weaver,	do.	60
	323	Rozael Woodworth,	do.	60
	324	Ezekiel Williams,	do.	15
	325	George Walter,	do.	30
	326	Thomas Ward,	corporal,	60
	327	Matthew N. Whyte,	cadet,	60
	328	John Walsh,	private,	30
	329	Kerly Ward,	do.	40
	330	John Younglove,	major,	72
	331	Gotfield Young,	corporal,	60
	332	John Yorden,	private,	30
	333	Nicholas Yorden,	do.	12
	334	Edward Shell,	do.	60
	335	Job Snell,	do.	15
	336	John Bogge, *alias* Bogue,	do.	60
	337	Dan Culver,	do.	60
	338	Elisha Fanning,	sergt. major,	30
	339	Silas Benton,	captain,	240
	340	James Crosslay,	private,	30
	341	James Gorman,	matross,	60
	342	John Philips,	corporal,	48
	343	Thomas P. Smith,	private,	60
	344	Danl. Cushman, (from Ver.)	do.	48
		Total of annual stipends,	. . . .	21,112 75

SCHEDULE OF PENSIONERS, continued.

District or Agency.	No. on the Roll.	NAMES.	Rank or Quality.	Annual Stipend.
New Jersey.	1	Josiah Burnet,	ensign,	$ 120
	2	William Broderick,	sergeant,	40
	3	Isaac Bennet,	do.	40
	4	John Burton,	private,	60
	5	Barnes Bunn,	do.	24
	6	Benjamin Bishop,	do.	24
	7	James Boden,	do.	30
	8	Thomas Carhart,	corporal,	60
	9	Robert Coddington,	private,	60
	10	Isaac Cotheal,	do.	60
	11	John Campbell,	do.	20
	12	William Crane,	lieutenant,	160
	13	George Compton,	corporal,	30
	14	Randolph Clarkson,	private,	30
	15	Morris De Camp,	sergeant,	48
	16	John Fergus,	private,	24
	17	Mahlon Ford,	captain,	240
	18	Daniel Guard,	private,	30
	19	John Griggs,	sergeant,	30
	20	John Hampton,	ensign,	72
	21	Theophilus Hathaway,	private,	60
	22	Jacob Hall,	do.	40
	23	William Howell,	do.	32
	24	Samuel Hull,	sergeant,	40
	25	Benoni Hathaway,	captain,	120
	26	Nicholas Hoff,	private,	60
	27	Patrick Hart,	do.	36
	28	James Jerolman,	lieutenant,	24
	29	William Jobbs,	sergeant,	60
	30	Richard Jones,	private,	40
	31	Francis Jeffers,	do.	24
	32	William Johnson,	do.	30
	33	Samuel Kirkendahe,	captain,	120
	34	Christian Kuhn,	private,	60
	35	John Ketchum,	do.	60
	36	Aaron King,	do.	40
	37	Samuel Lindsley,	do.	45
	38	Samuel Leonard,	do.	30
	39	Jonh M'Clure,	do.	60
	40	Peter Nefies,	sergeant,	48
	41	James Patton,	lieutenant,	159 96
	42	Jabez Pembleton,	private,	30
	43	Silas Parrot,	lieutenant,	72
	44	John Quinby,	private,	32
	45	Andrew Ross,	do.	16
	46	Daniel Snalbaker,	do.	60
	47	James Swift,	do.	60
	48	Michael Smith,	do.	60
	49	Samuel Stout,	do.	20

SCHEDULE OF PENSIONERS, continued.

District or Agency.	No. on the Roll.	NAMES.	Rank or Quality.	Annual Stipend.
New Jersey,	50	Aaron Stiles,	private,	$ 60
	51	James Sweeny,	do.	45
	52	John Scott,	do.	60
	53	James Thompson,	do.	60
	54	Josiah Tuttle,	do.	32
	55	Samuel Taylor,	corporal,	40
	56	Sylvester Tilton,	volunteer,	30
	57	John Williams,	corporal,	60
		Total of annual stipends,	. . . .	3,127 96

SCHEDULE OF PENSIONERS, continued.

District or Agency.	No. on the Roll.	NAMES.	Rank or Quality.	Annual Stipend.
Pennsylvania,	1	Ludwig Arbigust,	matross,	$ 60
	2	William Atkinson,	private,	45
	3	Daniel Aleshouse,	do.	20
	4	George Attender,	do.	60
	5	Luke Broadhead,	lieutenant,	108
	6	Thomas Blair,	do.	108
	7	Jacob Barnitz,	ensign,	120
	8	Daniel Baker,	private,	60
	9	Jacob Beatum,	do.	60
	10	James Brannon,	do.	60
	11	John Buxton,	do.	60
	12	Daniel Buck,	do.	60
	13	Philip Brenier,	do.	40
	14	Jonathan Burwell,	do.	30
	15	John Buskell,	do.	36
	16	George Burton,	do.	24
	17	William Boyd,	do.	60
	18	John Berry,	do.	30
	19	Michael Bowman,	do.	36
	20	William Bush,	do.	60
	21	Jacob Baker,	matross,	30
	22	John Brown,	sergeant,	40
	23	Jacob Baker,	artificer,	60
	24	Walker Baylor,	captain,	240
	25	Geoge Benedict,	private,	40
	26	Andrew Bartle,	do.	30
	27	John Cambis,	do.	60
	28	John Clark,	lieutenant,	96
	29	Thomas Campbell,	captain,	240
	30	Thomas Carney,	private,	36
	31	Charles Clark,	lieutenant,	160
	32	William Campbell,	sergeant,	48
	33	Adam Christ,	do.	21 32
	34	Robert Chambers,	corporal,	28
	35	Alexander Campbell,	mariner,	60
	36	William Congleton,	private,	40
	37	Alexander Caul,	do.	36
	38	Alexander Christie,	do.	36
	39	Daniel Callahan,	do.	30
	40	William Campbell,	do.	30
	41	John Cavanaugh,	do.	36
	42	John Cardiffee,	do.	60
	43	Josiah Conckling,	do.	30
	44	John Crawford,	captain,	240
	45	John Collier,	sergeant,	60
	46	Patrick Collins,	private,	60
	47	James Cooney,	do.	60
	48	James Correar,	do.	30
	49	Stephen Carter,	sergeant,	45
	50	John Durnall,	private,	36
	51	Patrick Dempsey,	do.	60
	52	Michael Duffey,	do.	40
	53	Henry Doyle,	do.	36

District or Agency.	No. on the Roll.	NAMES.	Rank or Quality.	Annual Stipend.
Pennsylvania,	54	Henry Dougherty,	private,	$ 16
	55	Anthony Dawson,	do.	32
	56	William Dewitt,	do.	30
	57	John Day,	do.	36
	58	William Deaver,	do.	40
	59	James Dowling,	do.	40
	60	James Dysart,	captain,	120
	61	Charles Daniels,	private,	60
	62	Samuel Doane,	do.	30
	63	Michael Drury,	do.	40
	64	Samuel Ewing,	ensign,	20
	65	James English,	sergeant,	60
	66	Joseph Elliot,	private,	40
	67	Benjamin Freeman,	sergeant,	36
	68	William Fegart,	private,	60
	69	Frederick Fultz,	do.	60
	70	John Francis,	do.	36
	71	John Fogas,	matross,	48
	72	Jacob Fox,	private,	20
	73	Patrick Fowler,	matross,	30
	74	Thomas Fream,	sergeant,	36
	75	John L. Finney,	sergt. major,	45
	76	Alexander Forsman,	captain,	120
	77	Thomas Gaskins,	lieutenant,	160
	78	Philip Gilman,	private,	48
	79	George Gerlack,	do.	36
	80	John Graaf,	do.	15
	81	Philip Gibbons,	do.	45
	82	Alexander Garret,	do.	45
	83	Sam. Gilman, *alias* Gilmore,	do.	30
	84	Jeremiah Gunn,	do.	36
	85	James Glentworth,	lieutenant,	80
	86	Alexander Gray,	private,	48
	87	Benjamin Hillman,	lieutenant,	120
	88	William Hebron,	sergeant,	60
	89	Valentine Hertzhog,	private,	60
	90	Philip Henry,	do.	60
	91	Patrick Hartney,	do.	60
	92	Jacob Hartman,	do.	60
	93	John Haley,	corporal,	45
	94	David Hickey,	private,	60
	95	Lawrence Hipple,	do.	30
	96	Peter Hartshill,	do.	30
	97	William Higginson,	do.	36
	98	David Haney,	do.	36
	99	John Harbeson,	do.	40
	100	James Irvine,	brig. general,	540
	101	Matthew Jack,	lieutenant,	160
	102	Thomas Johnson,	do.	60
	103	David Jackson,	private,	48
	104	Alexander Irwine,	do.	30
	105	William Johnston,	do.	48
	106	James Johnson,	do.	60

SCHEDULE OF PENSIONERS, continued.

District or Agency.	No. on the Roll.	NAMES.	Rank or Quality.	Annual Stipend.
Pennsylvania,	107	Andrew Johnson,	lieutenant,	$ 60
	108	John Kesler,	midshipman,	20
	109	Thomas Kelly,	private,	60
	110	George Kettle,	do.	60
	111	Robert Kearn,	do.	60
	112	Edward Kellen,	do.	36
	113	John Kincaid,	do.	60
	114	Benjamin Kendrick,	do.	40
	115	John King,	do.	48
	116	Philip Krugh,	dragoon,	30
	117	Nicholas Lott,	sergeant,	30
	118	Timothy Lemmonton,	do.	60
	119	Patrick Lush,	do.	60
	120	Samuel Lesley,	do.	48
	121	John Lalor,	private,	60
	122	Henry Love,	do.	60
	123	Isaac Lewis,	do.	48
	124	David Lyon,	do.	50
	125	John Leiby,	do.	20
	126	Miles Lewis,	do.	15
	127	Samuel Lee,	do.	30
	128	James Leonard,	do.	40
	129	Charles Lenox,	do.	60
	130	Judah Levy,	do.	60
	131	William Mackay,	captain,	240
	132	Kenneth M'Coy,	lieutenant,	66
	133	John Malony,	sergeant,	48
	134	John M'Gaughey,	corporal,	60
	135	Barney M'Guire,	do.	36
	136	Michael M'Annalty,	gunner,	60
	137	John M'Pherson,	midshipman,	32
	138	James M'Donald,	private,	60
	139	Hugh Moore,	do.	60
	140	John M'Gill,	do.	60
	141	Isaiah M'Carty,	do.	60
	142	Angus M'Ever,	do.	60
	143	Thomas Moore,	do.	60
	144	John Manerson,	do.	60
	145	John Modewell,	do.	60
	146	Ephraim M'Coy,	do.	60
	147	John Most,	do.	48
	148	Thomas Mayberry,	do.	48
	149	Samuel M'Clughan,	do.	48
	150	John M'Dermond,	do.	48
	151	Robert Montgomery,	do.	48
	152	James Mathers,	do.	48
	153	Jacob Miller,	do.	40
	154	Thomas M'Barney,	do.	56
	155	William Murphey,	do.	30
	156	Thomas M'Fall,	do.	30
	157	Thomas Monday,	do.	24
	158	Alexander Martin,	do.	50
	159	Joseph Moorhead,	ensign,	108

SCHEDULE OF PENSIONERS, continued.

District or Agency.	No. on the Roll.	NAMES.	Rank or Quality.	Annual Stipend.
Pennsylvania,	160	John Murry,	private,	g 60
	161	John M'Conehy,	do.	36
	162	William M'Kennan,	captain,	240
	163	James Moore,	corporal,	30
	164	Robert M'Clellan,	lieutenant,	52
	165	James M'Neal,	private,	60
	166	Matthew M'Connell,	captain,	180
	167	John M'Farland,	private,	16
	168	Josiah Magoon,	do.	60
	169	Robert M Kinney,	lieutenant,	156
	170	Dennis M'Knight,	private,	40
	171	Thomas Maze,	do.	21 42
	172	John Malony,	sergeant,	40
	173	John Neafas,	corporal,	60
	174	Christian Nagle,	private,	24
	175	William Nelson,	do.	60
	176	John Norcross,	do.	24
	177	Samuel Nesbit,	do.	60
	178	John O'Brian,	do.	24
	179	Joshua Peeling,	sergeant,	60
	180	Thomas Park,	corporal,	30
	181	Frederick Paul,	private,	36
	182	Abraham Pyke,	do.	20
	183	John Peirce,	do.	20
	184	Peter Parchment,	do.	40
	185	John Peoples,	do.	30
	186	Thomas Pearson,	lieutenant,	160
	187	Charles Plemline,	private,	36
	188	Andrew Pinkerton,	do.	39 64
	189	George Peirson,	do.	24
	190	Zachariah Reed,	do.	30
	191	George Richardson,	do.	48
	192	David Richey,	do.	30
	193	Jacob Rogers,	do.	48
	194	William Ritchell,	do.	48
	195	Jacob Rasor,	do.	40
	196	John Rybecker,	do.	48
	197	Griffith Rees,	do.	30
	198	John Rielly,	do.	48
	199	Nathan Rawlings,	captain,	120
	200	William Rice,	lieutenant,	80
	201	Christian Smith,	private,	60
	202	Jacob Shartel,	captain,	120
	203	Richard Scott,	private,	30
	204	Archibald Steel,	lieut. & adj't.	190
	205	Daniel St. Clair,	drum major,	60
	206	Bernard Slaugh,	private,	60
	207	John Saring,	do.	45
	208	Samuel Spicer,	do.	36
	209	John Stiller,	do.	20
	210	Henry Slotterback,	do.	60
	211	Bryant Sloan,	do.	30
	212	John Shultz.	do.	20

SCHEDULE OF PENSIONERS, continued.

District or Agency.	No. on the Roll.	NAMES.	Rank or Quality.	Annual Stipend.
Pennsylvania,	213	Joseph Sapp,	private,	$ 60
	214	John Stroop,	sergeant,	30
	215	Jonas Steel,	private,	20
	216	Abraham Storet,	lieutenant,	160
	217	Lazarus Stow,	do.	120
	218	Francis Smith,	private,	30
	219	William Stocker,	do.	36
	220	Peter Swartz,	do.	30
	221	Francis L. Slaughter,	do.	36
	222	Alexander Simonton,	sergeant,	36
	223	John Smith,	private,	30
	224	John Robert Shaw,	do.	60
	225	Christian Shockley,	do.	40
	226	William Stringfield,	do,	30
	227	Patrick Taggart,	sergeant,	48
	228	William Thomlinson,	private,	60
	229	John Taylor,	do.	60
	230	Francis Ticount,	do.	60
	231	James Tannehill,	do.	36
	232	Thomas Tweedy,	do.	60
	233	John Thompson,	do.	60
Per act Mar. 3, 1805,	234	Richard Taylor,	sergeant,	240
	235	Jonathan Tinsley,	private,	60
	236	Elias Utt,	do.	20
	237	Enoch Varnum,	do.	60
	238	Thomas Vanderlip,	do.	45
	239	Lewis Vaughan,	do.	40
	240	Edward Warren,	do.	60
	241	Jeremiah Wilson,	do.	30
	242	Philip Warner,	do.	24
	243	Charles Wallington,	do.	60
	244	Edward Wade,	do.	30
	245	John Wright,	sergeant,	30
	246	Caleb Warley,	lieutenant,	132
	247	George Wolfe,	private,	45
	248	Robert Wilson,	ensign,	30
	249	John Whittington,	private,	36
	250	Joseph Waters,	do.	60
	251	Francis White,	lieutenant,	80
	252	John Wood,	private,	30
	253	Andrew Wallace,	sergeant,	60
	254	Thomas Scotland,	do.	60
		Total of annual stipends,	. . . .	14,709 38

9

SCHEDULE OF PENSIONERS, continued.

District or Agency.	No. on the Roll.	NAMES.	Rank or Quality.	Annual Stipend.
Delaware, .	1	Edward Armstrong,	lieutenant,	$ 160
	2	Paul Boughman,	sergeant,	36
	3	Samuel Burchard,	corporal,	60
	4	John Clifton,	private,	60
	5	Isaac Carrell,	do.	60
	6	Peter Cunningham,	do.	40
	7	Patrick Colman,	do.	60
	8	William Dolby,	sergeant,	60
	9	Jenkins Evans,	do.	60
	10	Joseph Ferguson,	private,	60
	11	John C. Fabricius,	do.	48
	12	George Griffin,	do.	32
	13	Thomas Heldston,	do.	60
	14	Nelce Jones,	do.	30
	15	James Murphey,	sergeant,	60
	16	Joseph M'Gibbon,	private,	60
	17	Levin Pointer,	do.	60
	18	John Skilton,	do.	36
	19	Thomas Watson,	sergeant,	60
	20	Hosea Wilson,	private,	24
		Total of annual stipends,	. . . .	1,126

SCHEDULE OF PENSIONERS, continued.

District. or Agency.	No. on the Roll.	NAMES.	Rank or Quality.	Annual Stipend.
Maryland, .	1	Thomas Green Alvey,	corporal,	$ 22
	2	John Anderson,	private,	40
	3	Richard Anderson,	captain,	240
	4	John Brown,	sergeant,	60
	5	John Byrne,	private,	60
	6	James Burk,	do.	40
	7	James Blever,	do.	60
	8	Robert Barnet,	do.	40
	9	John Bennett,	do.	40
	10	Thomas Baker,	do.	40
	11	Charles Bucklup,	do.	40
	12	Thomas Bishop,	do.	40
	13	John Boyle,	do.	30
	14	John Bean,	do.	30
	15	Loory Benson,	captain,	240
	16	James Bruff,	do.	240
	17	Thomas Collember,	private,	40
	18	Peter Casberry,	do.	40
	19	James Current,	do.	40
	20	Edward Cain,	do.	30
	21	John Corbett,	do.	60
	22	John Craig,	do.	60
	23	Benjamin Coddington,	do.	30
	24	Charles Dowd,	corporal,	60
	25	Barnabus Doughty,	private,	40
	26	John Davis,	do.	40
	27	Lawrence Everhart,	sergeant,	60
	28	William Evans,	private,	40
	29	John Elliott,	waggoner,	30
	30	George Finleyson,	private,	40
	31	Dennis Flannaghan,	do.	40
	32	Philip Fisher,	do.	40
	33	Simon Fogler,	do.	20
	34	John Ferguson,	do.	60
	35	Benjamin Fickle,	lieutenant,	200
	36	John French,	matross,	60
	37	James Garsh,	private,	40
	38	John Gambare,	do.	40
	39	William Green,	do.	40 52
	40	Abraham Gamble,	do.	60
	41	Richard Harden,	sergeant,	60
	42	John Howard,	private,	40
	43	Samuel Huggins,	do.	40
	44	William Hurley,	do.	40
	45	Edward Hood,	do.	40
	46	Samuel Hinnis,	do.	20
	47	Samuel Harris,	do.	40
	48	Alexander Jones,	do.	40
	49	John Jonas,	do.	60
	50	James Isaacs,	do.	40

SCHEDULE OF PENSIONERS, continued.

District or Agency.	No. on the Roll.	NAMES.	Rank or Quality.	Annual Stipend.	
Maryland,	51	Benedict Johnson,	private,	$ 40	
	52	John Johnson,	do.	42	
	53	Robert Jenkins,	matross,	60	
	54	Richard Kisby,	private,	48	
	55	Robert Kearns,	sergeant,	60	
	56	John Kirkpatrick,	private,	48	
	57	Thomas King,	do.	36	
	58	Edward Kean,	do.	60	
	59	William Keough,	do.	60	
	60	John Lynch,	do.	44	
	61	Christopher Lambert,	do.	40	
	62	John Lowry, 2d,	do.	60	
	63	John Lowry,	do	40	
	64	John Lynn,	lieutenant,	200	
	65	Edward Leary,	private,	60	
	66	Jeremiah Mudd,	sergeant,	60	
	67	John Matthews	corporal,	44	
	68	John M'Coy,	private,	60	
	69	Michael M'Guire,	do.	40	
	70	Hugh M'Leod,	do.	40	
	71	John Mook,	co.	40	
	72	William Mooney,	do.	60	
	73	Cleon Moore,	captain,	180	
	74	Daniel M'Carty,	matross,	60	
	75	William A. Needham,	sergeant,	60	
	76	Roger Nelson,	lieut. cavalry,	200	
	77	James O'Hara,	private,	40	
	78	Joseph O'Guin,	do.	40	
	79	John O'Hara,	do.	60	
	80	James Pope,	do.	40	
	81	Joseph Polhemus,	do.	40	
	82	Christopher Reind,	do.	40	
	83	William Rogers,	do.	40	
	84	Charles Robinson,	do.	40	
	85	Michael Roe,	do.	40	
	86	Joseph Richardson,	do.	30	
	87	Joseph Russell,	do.	24	
	88	Christopher Reed,	do.	40	
	89	Jacob Redenour,	do.	60	
	90	John Repp,	do.	30	
	91	John Symmonds,	corporal,	60	
	92	Thomas Sherwood,	private,	36	
	93	James Scott,	sergeant,	24	48
	94	John Snyder,	corporal,	44	
	95	Thomas Saunders,	private,	40	52
	96	William Slye,	do.	40	
	97	Jacob Shanley,	do.	40	
	98	Philip Sullivan,	do.	40	
	99	John Shovell,	do.	40	
	100	Philip Shoebrook,	do.	40	
	101	James Smith,	do.	40	
	102	Daniel Smith,	do.	40	
	103	James Smith,	do.	40	

SCHEDULE OF PENSIONERS, continued.

District or Agency.	No. on the Roll.	NAMES.	Rank or Quality.	Annual Stipend.
Maryland,	104	David Smith,	private,	$ 40
	105	Joseph Smith,	do.	40
	106	Valentine Smith,	do.	40
	107	Valentine Smith,	do.	20
	108	James Smith,	do.	48
	109	James Sewall,	do.	60
	110	George Scoone,	corporal,	30
	111	Clement Sewall,	ensign,	96
	112	Richard Stedds,	private,	48
	113	James Tillard,	do.	40 52
	114	John Trisner,	do.	40
	115	Henry Tomm,	do.	30
	116	George Vaughan,	lieutenant,	160
	117	Nathaniel Wheeler,	private,	60
	118	John Wills,	do.	40
	119	Richard Wilkerson,	do.	40
	120	Mark Walsh,	do.	40
	121	James White,	do.	40
	122	Samuel White,	do.	60
	123	Michael Waltman,	do.	40
	124	James Watts,	corporal,	60
	125	Stephen Yoe,	sergeant,	60
	126	Thomas Yates,	private,	40
		Total of annual stipends,	. . . .	6,896 04

10

SCHEDULE OF PENSIONERS, continued.

District or Agency.	No. on the Roll.	NAMES.	Rank or Quality.	Annual Stipend.
Virginia, . .	1	James Askew,	private,	$ 40
	2	John Angill,	do.	40
	3	William Adkinson,	do.	40
	4	John Aikin,	do.	40
	5	Matthew Amicks,	do.	30
	6	Edward Absalom,	do.	60
	7	William Bradley,	sergeant,	60
	8	Robert Burchett,	private,	60
	9	Robert Beckham,	do.	50
	10	Lewis Belvin,	do.	50
	11	Benjamin Barber,	do.	40
	12	Alexander Bunton,	do.	40
	13	Bazel Brown,	do.	40
	14	Thomas Brown,	do.	40
	15	Alexr. Bonny, *alias* Bonnal,	do.	33 33⅓
	16	Francis Boyd,	do.	33 33⅓
	17	George Black,	do.	33 33⅓
	18	Thomas Booth,	do.	20
	19	William Butler,	do.	48
	20	John Bell,	lieutenant,	120
	21	Joseph Biggs,	ensign,	108
	22	James Braxton,	private,	48
	23	David Blew,	do.	40
	24	William Barber,	do.	40
	25	John Berry,	do.	60
	26	John Burton,	sergeant,	60
	27	Daniel Ball,	ensign,	120
	28	William Burke,	private,	40
	29	Samuel Burton,	do.	30
	30	James Buxton,	lieutenant,	48
	31	John Crookshanks,	private,	30
	32	George Cress,	do.	30
	33	James Campbell,	lieutenant,	100
	34	Thomas Clark,	sergeant,	60
	35	Bartlet Coxe,	private,	60
	36	Miles Cardiff,	do.	60
	37	Leonard Cooper,	captain,	166 66⅔
	38	James Cambers,	private,	60
	39	Francis Combs,	do.	50
	40	John Caldwell,	do.	40
	41	Archibald Compton,	do.	40
	42	Lawrence Corner,	do.	40
	43	James Cottman,	do.	33 33⅓
	44	John Corbett,	do.	20
	45	John Collings,	do.	15
	46	Henry Crook,	do.	40
	47	Thomas Coverly,	ensign,	120
	48	Isaiah Corbin,	private,	30
	49	John Crute,	lieutenant,	156
	50	Ischarner Degraffenreidt,	private,	60

SCHEDULE OF PENSIONERS, continued.

District or Agency.	No. on the Roll.	NAMES.	Rank or Quality.	Annual Stipend.
Virginia, . .	51	James Davenport,	private,	$ 40
	52	Abraham Davis,	do.	40
	53	Patrick Dougherty,	do.	40
	54	James Durham,	do.	26 66
	55	Joshua Davidson,	dragoon,	45
	56	Jonathan Dyer,	private,	60
	57	John Davis,	sergeant,	37 50
	58	Elijah Estis,	private,	40
	59	Reuben Earthen,	do.	26 66
	60	William Evans,	lieutenant,	96
	61	Crosby Foster,	private,	50
	62	William Francis,	do.	26 66
	63	Frederick Finder,	do.	26 66
	64	Thomas Fenn,	captain lieut.	200
	65	Albion Gordon,	qr. mr. sergt.	60
	66	Martin Griffin,	private,	50
	67	Patrick Glasson,	do.	40
	68	Joseph Gardner,	do.	33 33⅓
	69	Griffin Griffiths,	do.	40
	70	Paul Haggarty,	do.	40
	71	Benjamin Hoomes,	captain,	240
	72	John Hughes,	sergeant,	60
	73	William Hubbard,	do.	60
	74	Robert Hart,	drummer,	50
	75	Samuel Hunt,	private,	60
	76	Peter Howard,	do.	40
	77	John Halfpenny,	do.	40
	78	James Hamilton,	do.	33 33⅓
	79	Bartlett Hawkins,	do.	60
	80	Henry Hurst,	do.	30
	81	Elijah Hedges,	do.	60
	82	Fielding Harding,	sergeant,	'30
	83	Henry Hall,	private,	60
	84	John Holcombe,	captain,	180
	85	James Howard,	private,	30
	86	Richard Joy,	do.	50
	87	William Jones,	do.	40
	88	Thomas Jordan,	do.	40
	89	John Jeffries,	do.	36
	90	William Jones,	do.	60
	91	John Jordan,	lieutenant,	90
	92	Samuel Kirkpatrick,	private,	40
	93	Michael Kinson,	do.	40
	94	Robert Leonard,	do.	45
	95	Andrew Lewis,	do.	60
	96	Joseph Ligon,	do.	36
	97	Newman Landman,	dragoon,	40
	98	John Long,	private,	30
	99	Martin Murphey,	sergeant,	60
	100	James Murphey,	private,	60
	101	William Moore,	do.	60

SCHEDULE OF PENSIONERS, continued.

District or Agency.	No. on the Roll.	NAMES.	Rank or Quality.	Annual Stipend.
Virginia, .	102	John Morgan,	private,	$ 60
	103	John Morris,	do.	60
	104	John M'Clennen,	do.	40
	105	Richard Munay,	do.	40
	106	Joseph Miles,	do.	40
	107	Banks Moody,	do.	26 66⅔
	108	Andrew M'Guire,	do.	60
	109	Peter Mason,	do.	20
	110	William Morgan,	seaman,	48
	111	Simon Morgan,	captain,	240
	112	William M'Clannahan,	private,	30
	113	John Martin,	sergeant,	30
	114	John M'Chesney,	private,	40
	115	John Newman,	do.	60
	116	Abraham Nettles,	do.	40
	117	John Newman,	sergeant,	36
	118	Timothy O'Conner,	private,	40
	119	Dennis O'Farrall,	do.	26 66⅔
	120	William Overstreet,	do.	36
	121	Henry Overly,	do.	60
	122	William Peak,	sergeant,	60
	123	George Pitman,	do.	60
	124	William Parmar,	corporal,	50
	125	Thomas Philips,	private,	60
	126	George Pettit,	do.	50
	127	John Proctor,	do.	40
	128	Jacob Price,	do.	40
	129	John Powell,	sergeant,	40
	130	Robert Reading,	private,	60
	131	John Ryan,	do.	40
	132	James Rogers,	do.	40
	133	Charles Robertson,	do.	33 33⅓
	134	James Robertson,	do.	26 66⅔
	135	Nathan Rowland,	do.	20
	136	William Reading,	do.	40
	137	Peter Rust,	do.	33 33⅓
	138	John Rearden,	do.	40
	139	Daniel Rady,	do.	30
	140	Evan Ragland,	do.	36
	141	Thomas Rogers,	do.	30
	142	David Scott,	captain,	100
	143	John Seamster,	private,	60
	144	David Steele,	do.	60
	145	William Simmons,	do.	50
	146	Joseph Sandridge,	do.	50
	147	William Stricker,	do.	40
	148	John Smith, 7th regt.	do.	40
	149	John Smith, 8th regt.	do.	40
	150	John Stadner,	do.	40
	151	Smith Stephens,	do.	40
	152	Joseph Sears,	do.	33 33⅓
	153	Daniel Smith,	do.	48
	154	Samuel Swearingen,	do.	30

SCHEDULE OF PENSIONERS, continued.

District or Agency.	No. on the Roll.	NAMES.	Rank or Quality.	Annual Stipend.	
Virginia,	155	Benjamin Sadler,	private,	$ 36	
	156	Benjamin Strother,	dragoon,	40	
	157	Jacob Seay,	private,	60	
	158	Thomas Thweat,	captain,	240	
	159	Thomas Trent,	sergeant,	60	
	160	Thomas Thoms,	private,	60	
	161	James Taylor,	do.	40	
	162	Stephen Terry,	do.	40	
	163	John Thorp,	do.	40	
	164	William Tipton,	do.	60	
	165	Charles M. Thruston,	do.	240	
	166	Edward Tuck,	private,	36	
	167	Vincent Tapp,	sergeant,	30	
	168	Robert White,	lieutenant,	160	
	169	Willis Wilson,	do.	133	33⅓
	170	Hugh Wallace,	sergeant,	50	
	171	Jacob Wine,	private,	60	
	172	Robert Williams,	do.	50	
	173	Joseph Watkins,	do.	40	
	174	William Williburne,	do.	40	
	175	Jesse Witt,	do.	40	
	176	John Whitlock,	do.	40	
	177	Andrew Waggoner,	captain,	240	
	178	Joseph White,	private,	45	
	179	Henry Williams,	do.	60	
	180	John Yeager,	do.	50	
	181	Joshua Younger,	do.	20	
	182	John Yardley,	do.	40	
	183	John Carmichael,	do.	60	
	184	William Burke,	do.	30	
	185	James Batson,	do.	36	
	186	James Bridget,	do.	30	
	187	Daniel M'Carty,	do.	48	
	188	Reuben Plunket,	sergeant,	30	
		Total of annual stipends,	. . . .	10,340	14

SCHEDULE OF PENSIONERS, continued.

District or Agency.	No. on the Roll.	NAMES.	Rank or Quality.	Annual Stipend.
North Carolina,	1	James Ames,	private,	$ 60
	2	John Alverson,	do.	40
	3	George Bledsoe,	do.	60
	4	Isaac Bates,	do.	42
	5	John Baxter,	do.	36
	6	Charles Butler,	do.	36
	7	Thomas Belsiah,	do.	60
	8	James Christian,	do.	60
	9	James Christian,	do.	30
	10	Thomas Chiles,	captain,	160
	11	James Carrigan,	private,	36
	12	Samuel Carter,	do.	24
	13	Samuel Espey,	do.	30
	14	Charles Ellam,	do.	42
	15	David Flannagan,	do.	30
	16	Samuel Freeman,	do.	25
	17	William Fireds,	do.	30
	18	Herman Gaskins,	do.	40
	19	Joshua Gordon,	do.	36
	20	John Gillon,	do.	36
	21	Richard Grissum,	do.	36
	22	Thomas Goodrum,	do.	30
	23	Thomas Harris,	major,	180
	24	Elisha Hunt,	private,	60
	25	Wyat Hinckley,	do.	60
	26	James Houston,	captain,	180
	27	Daniel Houston,	private,	36
	28	Howell Harton,	do.	36
	29	Elias House,	do.	54
	30	Alexander Haynes,	do.	42
	31	William Hall,	do.	60
	32	John Huddleston,	do.	35
	33	David Johnson,	do.	60
	34	Francis Johnson,	do.	36
	35	Samuel Johnson,	do.	60
	36	Joseph Kerr,	do.	60
	37	Isaac Kennedy,	do.	36
	38	Elijah Kidwell,	do.	30
	39	James Larremore,	do.	30
	40	Amos Lewis,	do.	30
	41	Alexander Morrison,	sergeant,	60
	42	Daniel M'Kissick,	captain,	120
	43	Thomas M'Kissick,	private,	36
	44	Christopher Mourning,	do.	40
	45	David Miller,	do.	40
	46	James Porter,	do.	24
	47	James Potts,	do.	25
	48	Matthew Pitman,	do.	36
	49	James Parks,	do.	40
	50	Jesse Rigsby,	do.	40
	51	Humphrey Rogers,	do.	60
	52	James Redfern,	do.	36
	53	Michael Reep,	do.	30

SCHEDULE OF PENSIONERS, continued.

District or Agency.	No. on the Roll.	NAMES.	Rank or Quality.	Annual Stipend.
North Carolina,	54	John Sweeney,	private,	$ 60
	55	Thomas Smith,	do.	60
	56	James Smith,	do.	60
	57	Ithamar Singletary,	do.	15
	58	William Simpson,	do.	30
	59	William Smith,	sergeant,	60
	60	Hugh Stanley,	private,	40
	61	John Spears,	do.	36
	62	Philip Thomas,	sergeant,	60
	63	Matiah Turner,	private,	60
	64	Stephen Thomas,	do.	45
	65	Joseph Wasson,	do.	60
	66	John Wilson,	do.	30
	67	John Wilfong,	do.	20
	68	John Wentz,	do.	36
	69	Henry Williams,	do.	30
	70	Benjamin Vickery,	do.	36
		Total of annual stipends,	. . . .	3,389

SCHEDULE OF PENSIONERS, continued.

District or Agency.	No. on the Roll.	NAMES.	Rank or Quality.	Annual Stipend.
South Carolina,	1	James Armstrong,	private,	$ 16
	2	John Calhoun,	do.	21 42
	3	William Dunlap,	do.	21 42
	4	Robert Elder,	do.	40
	5	Joseph Gilmore,	do.	21
	6	Joshua Hawkins,	do.	36
	7	Malcom Keys,	do.	48
	8	John Looney,	do.	21 42
	9	Joseph M'Junkin,	major,	144
	10	Andrew M'Allister,	private,	21 42
	11	Daniel M'Elduff,	lieutenant,	159 96
	12	Samuel Otterson,	captain,	96
	13	John Martin,	private,	30
	14	Henry Weems,	do.	60
	15	Jasper Tommiton,	do.	30
		Total of annual stipends,	. . . .	810 64
Georgia, . .	1	William Andrews,	sergeant,	$ 60
	2	Herman Bird,	private,	30
	3	Daniel Conner,	lieutenant,	160
	4	Alexander Cameron,	private,	30
	5	Austin Dabney,	do.	60
	6	Charles Damron,	do.	60
	7	Thomas L Davis,	do.	30
	8	James P. Edmondson,	do.	50
	9	Benjamin Fry,	do.	60
	10	Thomas Green,	do.	30
	11	John Guthrie,	do.	30
	12	John Garner,	do.	30
	13	Thomas Henshaid,	do.	60
	14	Harrison Jones,	do.	50
	15	Henry Kerr,	captain,	120
	16	Seybert Odam,	private,	60
	17	Daniel Odam,	do.	55 68
	18	William Pentecost,	lieutenant,	50
	19	John Shackleford,	private,	40
	20	James Shirley,	do.	60
	21	Presley Thornton,	corporal,	30
	22	Samuel Whately,	private,	60
		Total of annual stipends,	. . . .	1,215 68

SCHEDULE OF PENSIONERS, continued.

District or Agency.	No. on the Roll.	NAMES.	Rank or Quality.	Annual Stipend.
Paid at the seat of government but residing in Kentucky,	1	William Little,	private,	$ 60
	2	Robert Barron,	do.	60
	3	Oliver Bennett,	do.	60
	4	Henry Shaw,	do.	30
	5	Squire Boone,	do.	36
	6	Quintin Moore,	do.	20
	7	George Fennell,	do.	30
	8	James Warson,	do.	40
	9	James Berry,	do.	20
	10	Isaac Burnham,	do.	48
	11	John Shanks,	do.	40
	12	Andrew Allison,	do.	36
	13	John Brown,	sergeant,	30
	14	William Nieves,	private,	30
	15	Thomas Hickman,	do.	24
	16	John Jacobs,	do.	60
	17	Robert Patterson,	colonel,	300
	18	Virgil Poe,	private,	30
	19	Joseph Shaw,	do.	24
	20	Joseph Todd,	do.	24
		Total of annual stipends,	. . . .	1,002
Tennessee,	1	Rinley Hazelet,	private,	60
	2	William Carr,	do.	30
	3	John Newman,	captain,	120
	4	Charles Killgore,	private,	30
	5	Joseph Reed,	do.	40
	6	Benjamin Blackburn,	sergeant,	60
	7	John Blair,	lieutenant,	96
	8	James Crawford,	ensign,	72
	9	Perry Floyd,	private,	30
	10	William Haile,	do.	20
	11	Ethelred Cobb,	do.	30
	12	John Kirk,	do.	30
	13	Samuel Newell,	lieutenant,	96
	14	John Taylor,	private,	45
	15	Thomas Wyatt,	do.	30
		Total of annual stipends,	. . .	789

SCHEDULE OF PENSIONERS, continued.

District or Agency.	No. on the Roll.	NAMES.	Rank or Quality.	Annual Stipend.
Paid at the seat of government but residing in Ohio, . .	1	Bartholomew Berry,	private,	$ 60
	2	Robert Williams,	do.	60
	3	William Wells,	captain,	240
	4	James Gillespie,	private,	48
	5	James Munn,	captain,	120
	6	Joseph Shaylor,	do.	240
	7	Humphrey Beckett,	private,	30
	8	Martin Rohrer,	sergeant,	45
	9	Edward Miller,	sergt. major,	60
	10	Daniel Fielding,	militia sergt.	39 96
	11	John Calhoun,	captain,	180
	12	George Adams,	private,	60
	13	Dennis Laughlan,	do.	30
	14	Younger Grady,	do.	36
		Total of annual stipends,	. . . .	1,248 96
Indiana territory, .	1	Robert Baird,	lieutenant,	120
Michigan, .	1	John Reynolds,	private,	36
District of Columbia,	1	Henry Carberry,	captain,	240
	2	Ambrose Lewis,	private,	45
	3	Henry M'Farlane,	do.	24
		Total of annual stipends,	. . . .	309

Aggregate payable at the Seat of Government.

Roll of Kentucky, . . .	$ 1,002
Tennessee, ...	789
Ohio, ...	1,248 96
Indiana, ...	120
Michigan, ...	36
Columbia, ...	309

Total annual stipends, seat of government, $ 3,504 96

RECAPITULATION.

District or Agency.	Number on the Rolls.	Amount of annual stipends.	Semi-annual payments.
New Hampshire, . . .	117	5.833 30	2,916 65
Massachusetts, ...	211	10,319	5,159 50
Vermont, ...	61	2,938	1,469
Rhode Island, ...	36	1,787 50	893 75
Connecticut, ...	192	9,778 50	4,889 25
New York, ...	343	21,112 75	10,556 37
New Jersey, ...	57	3,127 96	1,563 98
Pennsylvania, ...	254	14,709 38	7,354 69
Delaware, ...	20	1,126	563
Maryland, ...	126	6,896 04	3,448 02
Virginia, ...	188	10,340 14	5,170 07
North Carolina, ...	70	3,389	1,694 50
South Carolina, . . .	15	810 64	405 32
Georgia, ...	22	1,215 68	607 84

SEAT OF GOVERNMENT.

20 Kentucky, .	1,002			
15 Tennessee, . .	789			
14 Ohio, . .	1,248 96			
1 Indiana, . .	120	54	3,504 96	1,752 48
1 Michigan, . .	36			
3 District of Columbia,	309			
54	$ 3,504 96			

	Number on the Rolls.	Amount of annual stipends.	Semi-annual payments.
Total,	1,766	$ 96,888 85	$ 48,444 42

www.ingramcontent.com/pod-product-compliance
Lightning Source LLC
Chambersburg PA
CBHW060741280326
41934CB00010B/2303